animal attack!

BEAR ATTACKS

Patrick J. Fitzgerald

Children's Press
A Division of Grolier Publishing
New York / London / Hong Kong / Sydney
Danbury, Connecticut

To my wife, Wendy

Book Designer: Nelson Sa
Contributing Editors: Jennifer Ceaser and Robert Kirkpatrick

Photo Credits: Cover, p. 4 © Index Stock Photography, Inc.; p. 6 © Galen Rowell/Corbis; p. 9 © Index Stock Photography, Inc.; p. 11 © Ralph Reinhold/Animals Animals; p 13 © Victoria McCormick/Animals Animals; p 15 © Mark Stouffer/Animals Animals; p. 17 © Joe McDonald/Corbis; p 19 © Leo Keeler/Animals Animals; p. 20 © Raymond Gehman/Corbis; p. 23 © Index Stock Photography, Inc.; p. 24 © Paul A. Souders/Corbis; p. 27 © Animals Animals; p. 28 © Johnny Johnson/Animals Animals; p. 31© Animals Animals; p. 32 © Melissa Farlow/National Geographic Society; p. 35 © Index Stock Photography, Inc.; p. 37 © Melissa Farlow/National Geographic Society; p. 38 © Index Stock Photography, Inc.

Fitzgerald, Patrick J., 1966-
    Bear attacks / Patrick J. Fitzgerald.
    p. cm. – (Animal attack!)
    Includes bibliographical references and index.
    Summary: Discusses the history of bear attacks on humans and the reasons for the attacks, and includes information on loss of habitats for bears as well as species endangerment.
    ISBN 0-516-23312-2 (lib. bdg.) – ISBN 0-516-23512-5 (pbk.)
    1. Bear attacks – Juvenile literature [1. Bears]
    I. Title II. Series
    QL737.C27 F58 2000
    599.78–dc21

                                                    00-C24275

contents

introduction

In many ways, bears seem to be much like us. They can stand upright. They can be curious, playful, or angry. They are intelligent animals that can communicate with one another. Mother bears even spank their cubs!

Bears may look soft and cuddly. A wild bear is no teddy bear, though. Bears will attack if they are provoked. A bear also will attack if people come between the animal and its food.

The actual number of bear attacks on humans is very small. Bears usually avoid contact with people. In fact, people kill many more bears than bears kill people. Most bear attacks occur when people enter the bear's habitat. A habitat is an area where an animal naturally lives and grows.

You'd better hope you never see something like this!

The largest bear populations are in the national parks of the continental United States, Canada, and Alaska. These are the same parks that millions of people visit each year to go hiking and camping. People go to see wild animals in their natural habitats. Sometimes, people and bears will cross paths in these parks. When this happens, it can be dangerous for both bears and humans.

Bears cause millions of dollars of damage each year to people's property. Part of the fault lies with humans, who enjoy feeding bears. Most national parks and many communities have posted signs warning against feeding bears. This is because bears begin to associate humans with food. Bears looking for food will break into the cars, cabins, and tents of park visitors. Sometimes, bears that are searching for food will attack and even kill the people they encounter. Park rangers must protect hikers and campers from aggressive bears. Sometimes, rangers are forced to kill bears that have attacked or threatened humans.

Bears will break into campers' cars to get to food.

chapter one

THE BEAR FACTS

In the fall of 1984, Joel Larson had gone hiking near Mount McKinley in Alaska. As he returned to his car after the hike, he crossed paths with a mother grizzly and her two cubs.

Larson did something against which bear experts warn. He turned and ran. The mother bear chased after him. She knocked down Larson. Then Larson did something else bear experts say you shouldn't do. He tried to fight the grizzly. He picked up a log and attacked the bear. The bear bit down on Larson's hand. It lifted him up and slammed him onto the ground.

Then, the bear backed off and retreated into the woods with her cubs. As the bear looked back over her shoulder, Larson made yet another bad decision.

A bear can be ferocious if it is provoked.

He looked right into the grizzly's eyes. The bear turned and charged at Larson at full speed. Larson was knocked to the ground as the bear claws ripped into his chest and arms.

Normally, Larson would have been dead meat. However, this time he was lucky. For some unknown reason, the bear ran back into the woods. Larson got up and went for help.

Experts say the attack would not have happened if Larson had played dead. "Maybe I shouldn't have run," Larson told Scott McMillon, author of the book Mark of the Grizzly. *"But if you've got a 1,000-pound [450-kg] bear running at you, at a distance of about 30 feet [9 m], I'd like to see you just stand there. I'd like to see that."*

TYPES OF BEARS

There are eight different species (kinds) of bears. There are brown bears, American black bears, polar bears, giant panda bears, Asiatic black bears, sloth bears, spectacled bears, and sun bears.

Grizzly bears are a type of brown bear. Bears live in all parts of the world except Africa, Australia, and Antarctica. Only brown bears, polar bears, and American black bears live in North America. Sun bears, the smallest of the species, live in Asia.

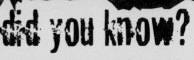

did you know?

Koala bears aren't really bears. They belong to a group of animals called marsupials. A marsupial has a pouch in which it keeps its young. The kangaroo is the best-known of all the marsupials.

BEARS OF NORTH AMERICA

Of the three species of bears that live in North America, the two most common are the black bear and the grizzly bear. Black bears and grizzlies have heavy fur coats that they shed each year. They carry a thick layer of fat under their skins. This fat keeps them warm in cold weather. Their front teeth are long and good for biting. Their back teeth (molars) are used to crush food. Grizzlies and black bears are carnivores (meat eaters), but they mostly eat plants and berries.

Most bears are solitary animals, which means that they like to live alone. However, they will communicate with one another by marking trees with their scent. To mark its scent, a bear will stand on two legs and rub its back, shoulders, and head against a tree. A bear uses its scent to tell other bears whether it is male or female. The scent also tells other bears that it is ready to mate.

Bears' mating season is in late spring or early summer. In winter, bears hibernate, which is a state resembling sleep. They make dens in caves, hollow trees, or holes in the ground.

Generally, bears are calm, quiet animals. Bears sometimes will growl when they eat or when they feel threatened. Bears may feel threatened when something invades their territory. A territory is an area that an animal lives in and defends.

A mother grizzly bear teaches her cubs how to find and catch food.

BEAR CUBS

Female bears can give birth to a litter of one to three cubs. Cubs are about the size of a small squirrel or chipmunk when they are born. They grow quickly by feeding on their mother's milk. They start to eat other foods after a few months. The cubs stay with their mother for several years. The mother bear teaches her young how to find and catch food. She also shows them how to stay safe.

Sometimes cubs walk away from their mother or get lost. Hikers may come across these cubs in the woods. If a mother bear thinks her cubs are in danger, she will try to scare the people away by growling. She may even attack humans to protect her young.

NATURAL ENEMIES

Because of their large size, bears have very few enemies. In North America, bears sometimes are killed by packs of wolves. In Asia, large tigers kill and eat brown bears and Asiatic black bears. Also, male bears sometimes kill cubs and female bears. No one is sure what provokes a male bear to kill its own kind.

Humans are the bear's greatest enemy. People kill bears for sport. They also kill bears and sell the bears' body parts. Some people use bear fur to make clothing and rugs. They make jewelry out of bear paws. They also use bears' gall bladders for medicine. It is against the law to hunt grizzly bears in the lower forty-eight states. In some states, it is against the law to hunt black bears as well. Unfortunately, some people still hunt bears illegally. Illegal hunting is called poaching. Poachers are the biggest threat to bears today.

Poachers kill bears for their
fur and other body parts.

chapter two

THE BROWN BEAR

It was 3:00 A.M. on September 24, 1995, when the grizzly attacked in Canada's Banff National Park. Susan Olin and Laurie Shearin were asleep in their tent. Suddenly, the huge grizzly tore into their tent. Shearin was sleeping with her pillow over her head. The bear ripped the pillow to shreds and tore into Shearin's arm. Then it bit Olin's arm and clawed her face and head. Olin fought back at first. Then she played dead. The bear stopped attacking the women and moved on to other tents.

In all, the grizzly mauled six people that night. Four of the bear's victims were seriously injured. Olin's facial wounds took more than fifty staples, and many rows of stitches, to close.

This hiker tries to get away from a grizzly by climbing a tree.

BEAR ATTACKS

Before the attacks, the grizzly had lived near a garbage dump. It had become used to eating food that had been thrown out. However, people did not want the bear hanging around the dump. The bear was moved to a national park. But this grizzly was not used to having to look for food. It targeted tents because they were the easiest places to find food.

Grizzly bears and brown bears are part of the same species. The name grizzly comes from the gray-streaked, or grizzled, hairs that brown bears grow as they get older.

WHY GRIZZLIES ATTACK

For many years, people have spun tales about grizzly bears being killers. Some of these stories have been based in truth. Grizzlies can be aggressive animals. Even a young grizzly bear can kill a person in a matter of seconds. However, most stories about grizzlies have been exaggerated. From 1900 to 1985, an average of less than 1 in 2.2 million visitors to North American national parks were injured in grizzly bear attacks.

People who are attacked by grizzly bears are rarely killed. Only about eighty people have been killed in North America by grizzly bears in the past one hundred years. Grizzly bears are not very interested in killing people. They are more concerned with defending themselves, their young, and their territory. However, a grizzly bear will strike out at humans if we give them a reason to attack.

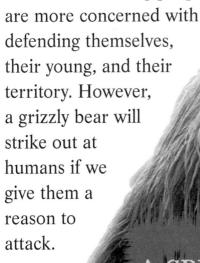

A GRIZZLY WILL ATTACK
IF A PERSON:
• enters into the bear's territory
• looks directly into the bear's eyes
• tries to run away from the bear
• goes near a mother's cubs

Hunters have wiped out much of the
grizzly population.

WHERE THEY LIVE

The brown bear is found in more parts of the
world than any other kind of bear. Brown bears
are found throughout North America, Europe,
and Asia. In North America, they are found along
the coast in Alaska, and Canada. Some of these
bears live on Kodiak Island near Alaska. They are
called Kodiak bears.

The Brown Bear

Some brown bears also live on the Japanese island of Hokkaido. Japanese news reported that on May 9, 1999, a bear killed a man in Hokkaido. It seriously injured two other people. That was the first fatal bear attack in Japan in nine years.

There are currently between 125,000 and 150,000 brown bears throughout the world. Grizzly bears are much more common in Canada and Alaska. Alaska has a total of approximately 40,000 grizzlies and Kodiak bears. The Canadian province of British Columbia alone has about 10,000 grizzlies.

Grizzly bears once lived all over western North America, from Mexico to Alaska. Bears used to live in every American state, except Hawaii. Hunters have almost wiped out the bear population in every state except Alaska. There are only about one thousand grizzlies left in the lower forty-eight states. They live mostly in national parks, such as Yellowstone Park in Wyoming. They also live in isolated parts of Montana and Idaho.

Brown bears are an endangered species. An endangered species is one that is in danger of becoming extinct (no longer existing).

did you know?

A bear that is standing on its hind (back) legs is probably just checking you out. When a bear gets down on all fours and puts its ears back, it is getting ready to attack.

WHAT THEY LOOK LIKE

The brown bear is the largest of the eight bear species. They can grow to be 10 feet (3 m) long. Adult grizzlies weigh about 900 pounds (405 kg). Some males can weigh more than 1,500 pounds (675 kg). This is twice as heavy as the largest male American black bears. Kodiak bears are the largest meat eaters living on land. They can weigh more than 1,716 pounds (780 kg)!

The brown bear has a heavy body with strong muscular legs. However, it is also a fast animal. It

The Brown Bear

can run up to 35 miles (56 km) per hour.

Brown bears are covered with a heavy, shaggy fur. Not all brown bears are brown. They can be black, cinnamon, red, blond, or a mix of these colors. You can tell the difference between brown bears and black bears by the hump. Brown bears have a muscular hump between their shoulders. Their front paws have large claws. These claws are large, strong, and slightly

Some grizzly bears stand 10 feet (3 m) tall on their hind legs.

curved. The length of the front claws can reach more than 4 inches (10 cm). Their claws help the bears to dig for food. Claws also can be deadly weapons in an attack.

WHAT THEY EAT

More than 75 percent of a brown bear's diet is made up of plants, berries, flowers, roots, and nuts of all kinds. Brown bears also eat fish, ants and other insects, and small animals. Sometimes they even eat moose and caribou. They also eat carrion, or animals that are already dead. Because of their large size, brown bears require a lot of food. During the summer, they will eat 80 to 90 pounds (36 to 41 kg) of food per day. During this time, brown bears are able to gain 3 to 6 pounds (1.5 to 3 kg) of fat each day. Bears need to bulk up to stay alive when food is scarce during cold winter months. They also need extra fat to keep alive when they hibernate.

Fish make up a large part of the brown bear's diet.

chapter three

THE BLACK BEAR

In 1997, Texas mother Patti McConnell was visiting the Liard River Hot Springs Provincial Park in British Columbia, Canada. She was hiking through the brush with her thirteen-year-old son and seven-year-old daughter.

Suddenly, a black bear leapt out of the bushes and lunged at the young mother. She was mauled to death in the park by a black bear as her two children watched helplessly. Other hikers saw the attack and threw sticks and rocks to scare off the bear. A hunter named Raymond Kitchen stepped in to try to stop the brutal attack. He was killed while trying to save McConnell. Kitchen was an experienced hunter who was familiar with the habits of

Black bears may look ferocious, but they are
usually afraid of humans.

*bears. His experience did not help him during this
attack. Kitchen died of claw and bite wounds to his
neck and chest.*

*Canadian officials could not explain the attack.
Black bears are normally afraid of people and rarely
are they known to attack humans.*

Black bears will break into cabins to find food.

NORTH AMERICAN BLACK BEARS

Black bears are the most common type of bear in North America. Yet fatal attacks by black bears are very uncommon. In North America, there have been only thirty-five fatal black bear attacks in the last one hundred years. The 750,000 black bears in North America kill less than one person every three years. Many more people die of bites from spiders, snakes, bees, and wasps. Also, almost no black bear attacks occur in national parks. Most attacks take place in remote wilderness areas.

Compared to grizzly bears, black bears are very timid (easily frightened). However, black bears do cause millions of dollars' worth of damage each year to campers' and hikers' property. They will break into cars, trailers, and cabins to get to food.

WHERE THEY LIVE

Black bears live in forests and national parks throughout North America. Some bears live as far north as the Arctic. Other bears live as far south as Mexico. In the United States, thirty-two states have American black bears living in their forests. Black bears are found throughout Canada, except on Prince Edward Island.

WHAT THEY LOOK LIKE

Black bears are smaller than brown bears. They do not have the brown bear's muscular hump. Most adult black bears are about 6 feet (2 m) long and weigh between 125 and 600 pounds (56 and 270 kg). The heaviest American black bear ever weighed was 805 pounds (362 kg).

The black bear is very quick. It can run at speeds of more than 25 miles (40 km) per hour.

Black bears are about half the size of brown bears.

Black bears are excellent tree climbers.

The curved claws on its front paws are far shorter than those of a grizzly. Black bears use their claws mostly for climbing trees.

The black bear's fur is usually black. However, the fur may be light brown, dark brown, beige, yellowish-brown, and even blue-white. Some black bears actually have white fur. These

did you know?

Black bears hardly ever growl. When they attack or eat their prey, they usually stay quiet.

bears are called Kermode bears. They live on islands off the coast of British Columbia, Canada.

WHAT THEY EAT

Black bears will eat almost anything. About 75 percent of their diet is plants, berries, roots, and nuts of all kinds. They eat carrion, fish, and insects as well. Black bears also may eat young mammals, including deer, elk, and moose. Black bears like to feed in the cool of the early morning or evening.

chapter four

THE FUTURE FOR BEARS

The history of bears and humans has not been a good one. Many people have seen bears as their enemies. Humans have hunted many bear species almost to extinction. Today, more bears die each year than are born. Some countries have recognized this danger. In the United States, grizzlies are protected under the Endangered Species Act.

Many governments have helped bear populations by setting aside wildlife preserves. Preserves are protected areas where people may not build homes, businesses, or highways. In these areas, bears and other animals can live safely.

The grizzly bear is protected under the Endangered Species Act.

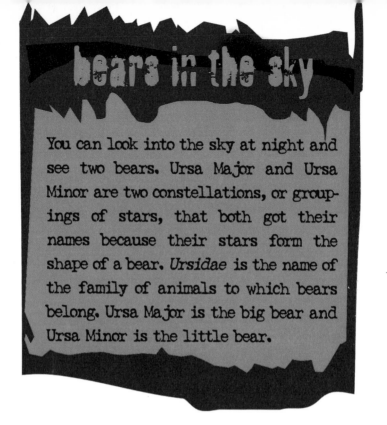

bears in the sky

You can look into the sky at night and see two bears. Ursa Major and Ursa Minor are two constellations, or groupings of stars, that both got their names because their stars form the shape of a bear. *Ursidae* is the name of the family of animals to which bears belong. Ursa Major is the big bear and Ursa Minor is the little bear.

Scientists are continually learning more about bears. They now know that bears are important to our wild regions. Because bears are predators, they eat prey and help keep the natural balance of animals in nature.

In the coming years, people must learn to respect bears instead of fearing them. People also must protect the fragile bear population. If human beings learn this lesson, both bears and people will be able to share the great outdoors.

Bears and people can learn to share their environment.

THINGS TO REMEMBER IN BEAR COUNTRY

Both black bears and brown bears can be aggressive toward humans. It is important to remember that these bears attack for different reasons. If you follow these rules, you will have a better chance of avoiding a bear attack:

- Always hike in groups. Never hike alone.
- Do not bring pets when you go hiking.
- Always make a lot of noise when you are hiking.
- Never go near a bear cub. Its mother will think you are threatening it.
- Never feed or pet a bear, especially a cub.
- Do not go near carrion. It might be a bear's meal.
- When camping at night, store food in a bag hanging from a tree. Do not keep food in your tent.
- Never stare directly into a bear's eyes.
- If you see a bear, turn around and slowly walk away.
- If a bear attacks you, do not try to run away. Bears move faster than humans.

FACT SHEET

Life spans: between fifteen and thirty years

Polar Bear
Ursus maritimus

**American
Black Bear**
Ursus american

Asiatic
Black Bear
Ursus thibetanus

Grizzly Bear
Ursus arctos

41

new words

black bear the most common bear in North America; also known as the American black bear

brown bear the largest of the eight bear species; the grizzly bear is the best-known brown bear

carnivore a meat-eating animal

carrion an animal that is already dead

cub a young bear

den where a bear sleeps

endangered threatened with extinction

extinct no longer in existence

grizzly bear a type of brown bear that is found in North America

habitat an area where an animal naturally lives and grows

hibernate a state of deep sleep that occurs during winter

Hokkaido Island the northernmost island of Japan, which is home to a species of brown bear

Kermode bears a type of black bear with white fur that lives off the coast of Canada

Kodiak Island island in Alaska that is home to the Kodiak bear, a large type of brown bear

marsupial a type of animal with a pouch to hold its young, such as a kangaroo or a koala

maul to attack and tear at

molars flat teeth in the back of the mouth used for crushing food

North America continent that includes the United States, Mexico, and Canada

poaching illegal hunting of animals

predator an animal that hunts and kills other animals for food

preserve protected land where people may not build homes, businesses, or highways

prey an animal that is killed and eaten for food

sun bear the smallest species of bear

territory an area that is occupied and defended by an animal or a group of animals

timid easily scared

resources

American Zoo and Aquarium Association
P.O. Box 79863
Baltimore, MD 21279
Web site: *www.aza.org*
This site has links to local and national zoos and aquariums and tells what each organization is doing to save endangered species. It also has information about AZA programs, how you can become involved, research links, and a photo gallery.

North American Bear Center
www.bear.org
Everything you would want to know about the American black bear. Includes answers to frequently asked questions (FAQs), photographs of bears, and a list of books on black bears.

The Cub Den

www.nature-net.com/bears/cubden.html
This site is dedicated to teaching people about bears and to helping bears and humans live together on Earth. It is especially designed for young Web surfers.

World Wildlife Fund—United States
1250 24th Street, NW
Washington, D.C. 20037-1175
Web site: *www.worldwildlife.org*
This site is dedicated to the conservation of endangered and threatened species. It includes the latest news about conservation efforts and information about their programs and how to get involved. It also sponsors the Conservation Action Network, an online chat room where people discuss conservation issues.

for further reading

Crewe, Sabrina. *The Bear* (Life Cycles). Austin, TX: Raintree/Steck-Vaughn, 1997.

Helmer, Diana Star. *Famous Bears*. New York: Rosen Publishing-PowerKids Press, 1997.

Hodge, Deborah. *Bears: Polar Bears, Black Bears and Grizzly Bears* (The Kids Can Press Wildlife Series). Buffalo: Kids Can Press, 1997.

Silverstein, Alvin, Virginia Silverstein, and Laura Silverstein Nunn. *The Grizzly Bear* (Endangered in America). Brookfield, CT: Millbrook Press, 1998.

Strasser, Todd. *Grizzly Attack* (Against the Odds Series). White Salmon, WA: Pocket, 1998.

index

index

ABOUT THE AUTHOR

Patrick Fitzgerald is a freelance writer who has had a lifelong interest in wild animals, including bears. He lives in Brooklyn, New York, with his wife Wendy, two cats, and a dog.